The 80/20 CFO

How to Make Strategic Transformations in Your Company

Janice Berthold & Suzy Taherian

The 80/20 CFO

Independently Published

Copyright © 2018, Jan Berthold & Suzy Taherian

Published in the United States of America

180620-01122-1-2

ISBN: 13: 978-1790707874

Here's What's Inside...

Introduction

The 80/20 CFO!

You may be asking yourself why this book is titled *The 80/20 CFO* and why it is co-written by someone who is not a CFO.

Allow me to explain. The 80/20 rule was formulated in the late 19th century by the Italian economist Vilfredo Pareto. The "Pareto Principle" came from his observation that roughly 80% of the effects come from 20% of the causes.

Likewise, only 20% of the work creates 80% of the outcome. While the numbers may not be spot on, the theory holds true in pretty much everything we do. This principle can apply whether you are working with a client, networking with potential investors, closing the books, or putting together a reporting package.

As the financial leader of your company, it's important to know, not only, what work results in bigger and better outcomes; but what work takes up the most time without providing the highest results. Our goal with this book is to provide the "Cliff Notes" to efficiently move the needle toward the biggest results for your business.

As mentioned earlier, I am not a CFO, but I have worked with many over the last 30 years. I have also started, and co-moderated four invitation-only CFO groups to improve results performance.

The CFO's job is one of the loneliest on the planet.

Our invitation-only groups help CFOs make better decisions, in part by, relieving the isolation they may feel when making important decisions. This process gives us the unique opportunity to provide them with unbiased opinions, so they stay focused on their key initiatives.

Lastly, I'm thrilled to be partnering with an amazing CFO, Suzy Taherian, an experienced CFO and adjunct professor of International Business at the University of California at Davis. I've observed her work with three different companies and witnessed the incredible results she gets.

Suzy is going to share her insights on important topics like, how to interact with the Board, how to sell change, how to partner with the CEO, and how to mitigate a company's exposure to risk.

We hope you enjoy the book!

It's not every day we are fortunate enough to have a successful CFO take the time to articulate the skills and strategies they use; to get more done by doing less and the secrets to looking like a hero while transforming your organization.

Sit back and listen as I interview Suzy on the mindsets she's cultivated and the game plan she's implemented, being a leader of strategic change within an organization.

Our hope is to inspire you to be a greatly successful CFO, to enjoy your work, with the goal of sharing what you learn along the way so you too can mentor those coming up. And, if this book helps you avoid some of the mistakes we made, then all the better!

To your success!

Jan & Suzy

What's Critical in the First 90 Days

Jan: Suzy, what do you recommend a new CFO do in the first 90 days, to set the stage for later success?

Suzy: Jan, that's a great question. When I look at a new job and begin organizing the first 90 days, I like to think of what a friend once said to me,

"What would Carlos say?"

I had just started a job in South America and on my very first day one of my new employees, Carlos, walked into my office and said, "I've been working in this company, at this location, for 15 years. I know the business. I know everyone and everyone knows me. I know the country and I speak the language. I really wanted this job, and yet they gave it to you. You don't know the country. You don't speak the language. Why did they give this job to you?"

It was a very awkward conversation, but I thought to myself, "He's right. I don't know why they gave me this job. He sounds like he's far more qualified than I am."

It was a good question, and I'm glad he asked it because I suspect everybody else was thinking the same thing. But Carlos was the only one who was direct enough and honest enough to say it to my face. It made me think, "What *is* it I bring to this job? Why was I selected for this position over other candidates?"

When I start a new position, I always think, "What would Carlos say? Why did they pick me for this job?" It makes me take a step back and focus, to ask myself "What are the needs of the organization, and the unique skills and abilities I have that can add value and make an impact? It's important to tie it back to the overall strategic goals: What are the key strategies of the company and how do I support those?"

Jan: How do you differentiate yourself compared to your predecessor?

Suzy: I focus on where the need is and leverage my unique strengths to quickly make an impact. When I've been hired as a new CFO, I've always gone in after very strong, qualified, hardworking CFOs, but the experiences and skill sets I brought were different than theirs.

Here's a great example. I was brought into a company where the CFO before me had been very strong in financing and banking relationships but had poor accounting and systems experience. They tried to implement a new accounting system but had failed. Their strategy was to improve operations by using the new accounting system to improve performance tracking and visibility. The biggest need they had was to fix the accounting system and get the financial reporting back on track, so that's where I put my focus.

In another situation, I came in after a very good controller-type CFO, but there was no one with banking and finance experience. A key strategic initiative was to grow the organization with additional investment They needed someone to do fundraising and bring in additional debt, as well as build banking relationships, so that's what I focused on.

Jan: How do you determine what are the key priorities?

Suzy: When I come into a job, I immediately seek stakeholder input. I talk to all the key stakeholders to better understand the strategic objectives and what they think the critical areas are. This gets me focused very quickly. I also ask them where they see my skill sets adding value and why they picked me for the role. This conversation is crucial to make sure I bring those experiences and abilities to the job.

The key stakeholders are the Board and the CEO. However, I also reach out and talk to the leadership team: head of marketing, head of legal, head of operations, the different critical leadership roles, to better understand what their perspective is and what they're looking for from the CFO, or what was lacking from the previous CFO. One of the most important steps at the initial stage is to quickly reach out to the stakeholders.

I also reach out within the financial organization to see who the controller or treasurer is. Sometimes I ask for the organizational chart to assist me with identifying who's who. Those are the people I talk to within the organization.

Something I learned from experience is that some important people are not at the top of the organizational chart, but they are thought leaders or major influencers, or have the historical perspective and institutional knowledge that can benefit me. I reach out to them to understand what's going on within the organization.

Jan: What is the objective in reaching out to the stakeholders?

Suzy: There are two key objectives in the conversations with stakeholders: 1) Getting input from the people who have been there and building an understanding of what they see the need is, and 2) Building credibility and relationships, which is the incubator for alliances; a crucial component in influencing change within an organization down the road.

I give them a sense of what my working style is and the experience I bring, I'm very open and curious to learn from them. Having this type of communication expresses that I have something to contribute, and, at the same time lets them know that I want and need their support. The key components here are the stakeholder engagement, aligning on the strategic direction, understanding the critical needs and what they think I bring to the organization, and building credibility.

Once credibility is established, it's critical to look for quick wins, because 90 days is not a lot of time. Coming into a new organization there are a lot of things we need to make happen. Therefore, if we can hit a couple of quick wins in the beginning, it helps build credibility and support for doing more beyond that.

Jan: That's sounds like a sound strategy, but how do you get those quick wins?

Suzy: One example I love to bring for getting quick wins is working with Heffernan, who has been a fantastic partner for me in building credibility. When I go into a new role as CFO, I always reach out to you, Jan, our insurance partner and say, "Look at our risk situation and tell me if it has been well-managed."

This technique has been a phenomenal success because your team at Heffernan comes in and gives me some great advice. Very quickly, I can identify areas of risk that had been missed, that could have been mitigated, and ways to save money in areas where we have been over-insured.

Within the first 90 days I now have a good assessment of our risk situation and can make an impact with some quick wins. This all spells credibility and gives me the support and momentum to accomplish other changes. That's been a great quick win for me.

Communicate the Quick Wins

By doing this you are letting people know what you bring to the table, what you plan to do, and how it's going to impact the organization. As we hit those milestones, they see what we are trying to deliver is delivered. This helps the new CFO build trust within the organization as we go forward. A lot is happening in those first 90 days, but it all goes back to the question, "What would Carlos say? What would Carlos ask me," and trying to answer the implicit question within the organization, namely, "What's this new CFO capable of doing, and why would they select her for the role?

Jan: By the way, how did the story with Carlos turn out? Were you successful in that organization?

Suzy: Carlos and I became good friends, and his guidance as a stakeholder was invaluable. I learned from him that the company had been very inward-looking for many years, and a key strategic initiative for that company was to leverage global best practices around the world at other companies in order to build a world-class organization. The unique skill I brought was my extensive international network and my understanding of financial processes in other locations and other companies.

Set Key Performance Metrics

I quickly reached out to contacts in other countries to develop a list of 16 key metrics to drive our performance. Based on my research with other high-performance companies, we set challenging targets for each metric. We started closely tracking the metrics and celebrating successes weekly. Quickly the organization began to see how it compared to other companies in other parts of the world and how we were making measurable progress towards becoming world class. While results improved, I was very pleased to see that morale and productivity improved as well. With clear quantified objectives, employees were getting recognition for delivering on impactful activities so they focused on high priority activities. This eliminated frustrations with wasted time and efforts on non-core activities. Overtime hours went down. Our company quickly gained recognition for its high-performance culture. I was able to secure promotional opportunities for several team members, including Carlos, in other global assignments. Today Carlos is still a good friend and he's actually in my former job, the position that he had always wanted.

Jan: Clearly setting up the right metrics was really important in quickly driving performance in the first 90 days. Numbers and metrics and analysis are important to all CFOs. But as you mentioned, dialogues with key stakeholders are also critical in those first 90 days. How do you prioritize whether to focus on analysis or reach out to talk to people?

Suzy: Analysis gives the insight on where the problems are; talking to people builds the consensus to solve those problems. Many CFOs tend to be very strong in analytics and financial analysis, so they will ask for the numbers and sit in their room pouring through the financial data. This *is* helpful, but there's a lot of stuff buried in there that may not pop out at them.

Without having all the conversations I covered earlier, they may be missing the critical needs within the organization. They're also missing building those relationships and getting buy-in and letting people know about themselves and their credibility. They are missing a golden opportunity.

In one case, when I was the new CFO, the person before me had not reached out within the organization, so people came to me and said, "We didn't know this person, we don't know how they made decisions. We didn't always support what they did because we didn't know where it came from."

I realized the person before me had been a brilliant mind but hadn't done a good job of building relationships. When they went to take the initiative and act, there was no support from within because people may not have agreed with them on the high priority items or understood where the decision was coming from.

The natural tendency for many CFOs is to bury themselves in their office and stare at the numbers. A much more effective strategy is going out and talking to the stakeholders to build credibility and relationships. If you don't get that accomplished you will be attempting to make a change within the organization, without support or credibility, and that makes it very, very tough.

That's why I have seen a lot of CFOs fail and exit very quickly. If you see a CFO who's only been there a year or two and is then asked to leave, it's often because of that. They came in and tried to change something that didn't need to be changed, or something did need to be changed, but people weren't aligned with them on that goal. The poor CFO ends up being out on a limb by themselves.

Helping the Board be an Effective Coach

Jan: What recommendations do you have for interacting with the Board?

Suzy: The relationship with the Board is like the roles in a football game. The Board is the coach; the CEO is the quarterback; my role as CFO is part statistician (to provide the analysis and data of the plays they're considering), and part cheerleader, to bring everyone together around a shared vision and push to persevere to realize it. The role is also part announcer, to update key stakeholders (shareholders or analysts) on the successes and how the team is progressing towards the end zone.

It's important to have the Board align around a key vision and clearly communicate that to the CEO and CFO. Then the executive team and the Board should align on the strategies to achieve that vision. The whole team should be working off the same game plan. What I find useful is to build a relationship with the Board by using a strategic planning process.

Strategic Planning Process as a Board Alignment Tool

Anywhere I've gone, I've encouraged the organization to go through a strategic planning process. And that means asking the hard questions:

- What are we going to do in the next three to five years?

- What's our assessment of the current market?

- What's our assessment of the future market?

- What's our competitive strength, and our ability to grow and beat the competition?

It's a great way to have a dialogue with the Board and to understand what their vision is, where they see the organization, and how they want to challenge it. That's a very natural conversation and the outcome is very good. But the process is also good because it helps alignment to occur; everyone's on the same page, where they want to go, how fast they want to get there and how they want to get there. It also limits wasted energy on minor topics that don't have strategic impact.

Jan: You mention asking the hard questions from the Board of Directors. Why are these questions difficult? How do you help the Board align on the answers?

Suzy: To be effective, a good Board should have a diversity of opinions; but that sometimes makes it difficult to get alignment. Open communication is a great way to build a relationship with the Board. It's not always an easy quick conversation. Different Board members bring different experiences and may have different agendas. Sometimes different Board members have different perspectives and it could be different from what the CEO wants to do.

The Data will Show the Way

To help the Board and CEO align on the right strategies, my role is the statistician: I make sure everyone has the same data. Good analysis can help clarify which strategies have a higher probability of success. The insights about the organization's performance can help the Board make better strategic decisions and ultimately, they'll be better at coaching the team.

During the 2008 global financial crisis, I developed detailed financial models for our $4 billion organization. It was a dynamic model so I could meet with the Board and test different scenarios and sometimes model the outcome in real time. I also try to make sure I come with different proposals so the Board and executive team can consider some alternatives. Robust market and competitive data are also helpful so they can stress-test the plan.

In my announcer role, I keep the board abreast of our progress or obstacles so they can determine if we need to fine-tune our game strategy. During those turbulent days, I was giving weekly updates to the CEO and the board. We would have to make adjustments to our plans as we saw key changes in the market. We tracked leading indicators to predict financial outcomes and make decision quickly.

And as cheerleader, I'm supporting the CEO, our quarterback, to believe we can achieve the goal. The CFO is often the sounding board for the Board and CEO. We need to listen and give positive reinforcement. This can be difficult for many CFOs as we tend to be risk-averse with strong analytical skills so we can quickly identify the risks in any situation. While the Board appreciates that objectivity, it can come across as pessimistic over time. One way to address that is to identify the problem but also recommend a solution.

Don't say why it won't work; advise how it could work

In one situation, the Board asked me to evaluate a potential strategy to launch a new technology with a $100 million investment. My analysis showed that it would be unprofitable. But instead of going back to the Board with that bad news, I redid the analysis with different assumptions, such as pacing capital expenditures with modular design, minimizing overhead, leveraging other technology, putting laser-focus review on cost and pricing assumptions, identifying government incentives for R&D, looking at possible tax advantages, exploring creative financing options, etc. I even contacted some financing sources to validate the assumptions. I presented the final analysis and showed what was possible. The Board was very pleased and we shifted strategy towards the alternative approach.

I find if we get everyone through the strategic planning process and provide good analysis to get everyone aligned, it reduces the questions and friction down the road. It's a very useful process.

Ultimately, the Board, the CEO, and the CFO are working together in their different roles to drive strategy for the company. The strategic planning process helps clarify the roles and keeps the focus on driving strategy.

Inspiring the Talent on Your Team

Jan: How do you assess and manage your team?

Suzy: This is one of the things we do really quickly when coming on to a new team, and my story on this is what I call…

Find Dave in Minnesota

When you come to a new organization, you inherit a team. I get the organizational chart so I know who's who and I try to meet with the team on a weekly basis. I put together some Key Performance Metrics to give my team a way to communicate with me and to know how I measure their performance. I try to connect their performance metrics with the strategic objectives. We're always trying to keep the organization focused on the strategic direction; tying performance feedback and accountability to strategy is a great way to align the team and set the right incentives.

It helps define their roles, "Here are the key objectives, here are the key metrics, and here's what I expect you to do." It not only guides each team member to better understand their role, but it also helps me assess their performance against those goals. I find that sometimes the formal processes and formal organizational charts may hide unsung heroes.

This is where Dave in Minnesota comes in.

In every organization there's a guy like "Dave in Minnesota." I discovered him a few years ago. In this particular organization, the accounting system wasn't working well, and as a result we were suffering. The operations folks didn't know how they were doing because the accounting system wasn't working.

I had a comptroller and a treasury person, but the comptroller quit, so I was stranded with no accounting system and no comptroller. I was running blind. But as I talked to different people in the organization, they kept saying, "Well, call Dave in Minnesota. He's got some good numbers."

I heard the same thing from a few different people, but they said it was not our biggest location. We had plants all over the country, and Minnesota was a smaller office. Dave didn't show on the organizational chart as a senior person.

But I did call him and found out very quickly that Dave, out of his passion and interest, had methodically and consistently been tracking the data across all the plants for several years.

He had spreadsheets tracking production data, cost data, revenue data, and pricing. It was amazing how much data analysis this guy had. He intentionally had a full, robust accounting system he was running outside of our normal accounting system, which wasn't working.

He was a brilliant guy. He didn't have the kind of pedigree you'd normally expect for a senior finance person, but he was incredibly smart, hard-working, very knowledgeable, and very well-respected within the organization.

I talked to Dave and found myself relying on him more and more. When we put in a new accounting system, we validated the data in our accounting system with the figures in Dave's spreadsheets. It's not common to find somebody with a trove of data, but I found it's very common to find people within the organization who are unsung heroes who have done great work or have institutional knowledge who are severely undervalued.

I offered him the job as comptroller in California. He said to me, "Suzy, I don't want to move to California, my family's here." I said, "Okay, fine. Work from Minnesota, and we'll do it virtually. Fly in one week a month to California." We gave him a raise and it worked out well for the organization because the cost of living in Minnesota is much lower than in California.

Here's the great thing. Without paying a recruiter fee, without paying a relocation fee, we had found someone within the organization who could step into the comptroller role. It was a bonus that he had the trust of the organization and for a lot less cost than if we went out and recruited a person in California. Dave was a lifesaver.

Jan: How do you connect with your team?

Suzy: My beginning protocol always include:

- Chatting with people across the organization so I can meet as many people as possible informally. I like team lunches or one-on-one lunches to get to know them and build relationships.

- Having weekly meetings so I can get good insights from people I'm working with, more formally. Like most CFOs, I'm data-driven and like performance metrics so weekly meetings are great for tracking data and quantifying progress. It gives a team an understanding of my workstyle.

- Looking for people I can promote from within to recognize high potential strong performers. Often organizations will be nervous with a new CFO because he or she will bring in their own team and replace the existing players. I want my team to know I acknowledge strong performance within the incumbent team.

As I give more metrics and organize clear and quantifiable goals and responsibilities, it quickly becomes obvious who are the strongest performers, as in the case of Dave from Minnesota, who've been undervalued and pull those folks up.

This is great when you're coming into a new team to find team members with institutional knowledge and promote within the organization.

Jan: How do you determine if you need external hires and what you're looking for in those candidates?

Suzy: In staffing, one of my key goals is to make sure the people we have are consistent with our strategy. In one organization, for example, our strategy was to be a low-cost manufacturer of a standardized product.

The key differentiation for us was our employees were nicer to work with than a much larger competitor who was stodgy, arrogant, and difficult to approach. In this strategy, it made a lot of sense for us to recruit young people out of college to fit our low-cost strategy, so we could train them.

They were very eager and hardworking, but because they were young and trainable, we had a very approachable, customer-friendly style. Because our product was simple and basic, it was easier to train them very quickly. In this case, we focused on people with good attitudes and customer-friendly skills.

In another company I worked with, the product was very complex and required many years of experience. In this particular industry, if you didn't have those years of experience, it was hard to be taken seriously.

Earning customer and team member trust was very important. We relied on experienced individuals who commanded higher pay. This was expensive but their technical expertise was important and fit our strategy. It's important when considering staffing to *understand what your strategy is* and *what kind of people to bring in within the organization.*

Getting Comfortable with the Financials

Jan: This is great knowledge. What helpful tips can you recommend to help a new CFO get comfortable with the financials?

Suzy: This is a tough one. You're coming in quickly, so how can you assess the financials? I'm going to tell you a story about…

Looking for *Alquilar*

Alquilar is the Spanish word for rent. When I showed up for a new job in South America, I said we must report our leasing activity on an annual basis. I asked our team, "Do we have any leasing?" They said, "No, we don't have any leasing." I said, "Strange, I just rented an apartment and my contract said *alquilar*, which means to rent or to lease."

I saw in our plans a lot of *alquilar*, meaning we were leasing stuff. But I was told, "No, no, *alquilar* means to rent, we're renting things, we're not leasing things." They were translating the vocabulary differently. I said, "Well, you know, in accounting, it doesn't matter if the contract name is lease or rent. If the content is a lease, we have to report it as a lease."

It turned out we had over $100 million in leasing.

My thought process there is when I come in, I look for *alquilar*. I look for the places where the accounting rules can be different or complicated so there may be misinterpretations. These are the hot spots.

There are certain accounting areas that are complicated, especially between different accounting systems. US GAAP and Argentina GAAP can be different. This is in leasing, this is derivatives accounting, inventory accounting, purchase accounting, depreciation; these are some of the problematic areas, and I know usually if I investigate these areas, I will find there are accounting challenges.

If there's a person who's been in the role a long time, those are high-risk areas.

Typically, the accounting rules have changed, or the business may have changed, but people tend to do the work the same way they've been doing it year after year. That's a good place to probe to make sure we've kept up. Whenever there have been accounting changes or new rules, it's good to check to see if we have complied with the changes.

I try to poke in the areas which I think are hot spot areas, trying to find the red flags and look for places where there might be misinterpretation.

Jan: Where does the audit procedure come into play?

Suzy: Before I take a job, I always ask for the audit reports. This is my secret weapon. When auditors have finished with a company, they produce a report that goes only to the Board, not to the public. Since it's a private report, the auditors will often be quite candid in that report and include observations that would not be included in the official audited financials. The CFO has access because it is such a powerful tool it gives you a sense of where the auditors saw weak spots or special opportunities for improvement. These are very helpful.

But I don't rely on these audits solely.

One company I worked with received a clean bill of health from the auditors. It even passed a very rigorous Sarbanes-Oxley testing. But when I looked closely at the inventory accounting, it was off by $6 million for the last five or six years, and nobody had noticed it. I like to get the auditor's report, and I always go through everything myself.

The Power Tool: Budget-Versus-Actual

Another process I've found very helpful for going through the deep dive accounting is to do the budget-versus-actual variance analysis. It's a great way to see how the company is progressing toward strategic milestones and budget targets. And at the same time it allows you to review and check the accounting.

I pull the team together at the end of the close and sift through the report by region or by budget owner, line by line, and go through budget-versus-actual.

This gives me two good pieces of information.

- It gives me an idea of what the budget is and if we're tracking to it, and why or why not.

- And if we've made an error in accounting, it'll pop up.

If we're missing the budget by a lot, we'll ask the question have we double booked an entry or missed an accrued or something? Budget-versus-actual review process brings a good discipline to the organization. It forces the management team to understand their budget and realize they will be held accountable for it each month. It reinforces the budget which should tie to the strategic plan so it assures the organization is moving in the right direction.

For a new CFO, a budget-versus-actual process review is very helpful to do month by month, line by line. After a few months it can get a little bit quicker in the process, but in the initial months, it's helpful.

It's the budget-versus-actual variance analysis of what happened last month, but over time it translates into a forecasting tool. You can say, "Okay, this is what happened last month. We missed the budget by $100,000. What are we doing this month to change it? How are we going to get back on track, or are we going to get back on track?" It also becomes a great tool for forecasts. The monthly conversation helps drive performance improvement and strategic alignment.

I find getting the auditors' report, looking through the financials myself for the red flags and hot spots, and budget-versus-actual has been very helpful in getting comfortable with the financials.

Jan: Do you have an example you can share that illustrates that?

Suzy: Certainly. In one location we had plants across the country, and I started doing the budget research with each plant.

The first thing I discovered was that they didn't know what their budget was, so once they knew that information we had ground to play on. After we did this some accounting errors popped up, so we corrected those. By doing this it became clear where we were consistently missing numbers.

It wasn't an accounting problem; it was an operational issue. From there, I could translate into what operational strategies were needed to improve the accounting to get better results.

For example, if I found an error in the inventory accounting I met with all the operational leaders inside the inventory team and explained to them how inventory accounting is done. I said to them, "If you take these different operational strategies, this is how it's going to translate into a financial result and your financial performance." I gave them an idea of how to make decisions that would impact their financial results. I've also done this with sales strategy and revenue recognition, in order to help the operational folks understand accounting. This helps them know how they're going to be measured. It's incredibly powerful.

Optimizing Across the Organizational Silos

Suzy: CFOs can make a big impact by looking across the organizational silos and taking the enterprise-wide view. Here's a good example of where I reviewed the budget versus actual reports by region and noticed a big synergy that each region had missed, I noticed we were losing money in two regions that bought material from the same supplier. We had two regions, northern California and southern California, and both regions were buying from the same supplier.

We had a long-term contract to buy from the supplier. In northern California, our plant had a very high-cost structure. In this situation, we should be buying cheap material because if we bought materials for $40 a ton and ran through a plant another $40-a-ton processing, it would cost us $80 a ton to produce product. But we were only selling it for $65 a ton, which meant we were not making money.

We should be buying material at $20 a ton and processing it at $40 a ton.

I went back to them and said, "Your supply numbers are wrong. We can't change the way the plant is structured. It is what it is. The processing fee is not going to change, but you could stop running this expensive material through the plant because we're losing money on every ton we process."

On the flip side of that, in southern California we had a plant that operated at a very low cost which could run for $20 a ton, which would enable us to buy higher quality material at a higher price. But the plant had very low utilization and was only running one shift, which meant we were losing money because we weren't covering our fixed cost. I asked, "Why don't you buy more material and run a second shift? That way you can afford to pay up to $40 per ton for material and should be able to find plenty of supply at that pricing for a second shift?" They replied, "We don't have any more supply, this is all the supply we can get in the market." I said, "Well, that's a lost opportunity because if you ran the plant at full capacity, instead of at just 50% utilization, shift by adding a second or third shift, we'd obviously make a lot more money."

In northern California we had too much supply, in the southern part of the state we didn't have enough supply, and both were locked into the same supplier contracts.

Each plant manager was running their respective plant, with their plant-specific limits and optimizing within their plant. They were not looking across the enterprise and trying to optimize across the silos.

I said to the northern California plant manager, "Why don't we go to the supplier and tell them instead of sending the supply to northern California, why not send it all to the southern California plant? That way we wouldn't have to lose money by running the supply through the northern California plant. With the additional supply, the Southern California plant could run it at a much lower processing cost; then they could add a second and third shift and we could significantly improve utilization."

We called the supplier and said, "We'll honor our commitment to you, but send it all to southern California. The pricing's still the same." The supplier had no problem with our strategy.

When we did that it was like we flipped a switch. Suddenly, the northern California plant went from losing money to making money because they weren't running unprofitable volumes. The southern California plant could now add second and third shifts and be fully utilized.

The company went from two unprofitable plants to two profitable plants without having the supplier change the terms of the agreement. This is the gold you find when you get into conversations with the operations people and understand budget-versus-actual; you need the details of how the business is running.

What does their offering or supply cost? What is their pricing? By doing this we can get into operational decisions that can help two businesses go from taking a loss to making a profit.

It's all about getting comfortable with the financials, by looking for *alquilar*, and finding the hidden anomalies and missed opportunities.

Initiating Change in Your Organization

Jan: That's a great turnaround. How do you make changes in the organization?

Suzy: Before making a change in the organization, it's important to know what your situation is.

Does the patient have a heart attack or is it indigestion? Therefore it's important to have a physical engagement to understand what the key issues are. The reason I say this is, before you can make changes, you have to understand what the problems are and how much support there is for change. If you come into a situation with a heart attack, there is a need and urgency for immediate action, and the Board and the stakeholders will want you to take some action right away.

If its indigestion, then they'll support changes, but they're looking for slower changes, a little bit more buy-in required and more gradual incremental changes.

That's the important thing - first understand the severity of the situation.

When I came into one organization, it was the one I talked about where the accounting system had crashed. They didn't have an accounting system. They hadn't been able to send bills to their customers to get paid, so they had no cash. Since they had no cash, they hadn't been able to pay the vendors. The customers aren't happy because they're not getting bills, they have no idea how much they owe. Vendors are unhappy because they haven't gotten paid in a couple of months. The Board is unhappy because they have no financials; they don't know how their organization's doing. The morale of employees was terrible because customers and vendors and the Board were yelling at them.

Resuscitating a Business

This was a complete heart attack situation. The good thing about the situation is, as a CFO, you get a lot of leeway to make changes. I came in immediately and said, "Okay, the first thing we need to do is to get some cash to pay bills." I went in with the Board's support and slammed in a line of credit.

Next, we needed to fix the accounting system. I hired a bunch of temps, got the Board's approval, and put in a new accounting system ASAP. The third thing we needed to do was to call the vendors to make sure our suppliers would stand by us while we went through this transition. I got a list of top-300 suppliers and called every one of them and said, "I'm the new CFO. I apologize for the mess we're in. Here are the things I'm going to do. Bear with me. I'll get back to you. If you have any questions, please send it to this email box, and I'll respond to you at night whenever I have time." During the day, I was running around trying to fix things.

At the same time, I looked for a way to reduce costs. Since we had a cash flow issue, we wanted to make sure we weren't using the critical cash on stuff that didn't make sense. Very quickly, we put in a new accounting system; we put in a new line of credit. I went back to the Board once I got the accounting system and said, "Now I have the financial reports, it's clear the business needs additional equity. The cash flow situation is bad, and here's my forecast and here's how much money we need." Then, we went out and raised money and got conditional equity in the business, so we could support it.

Then I said, "Here are the cost issues I'm going to fix." You can't go in and say, "Give me more money," without saying what you are going to do for the business. We had a good conversation with the executive team and presented an overall strategic plan. It included plans for growth and the funding we'd need for that. It also included recommendations for cost reductions and efficiencies we could achieve immediately.

With the Board's ok, I started executing immediately. I said, "Okay, we need to cut costs," and we restructured and reduced some of the corporate overhead positions. We relocated the corporate headquarters to a lower cost area. I looked at all our various key service providers like auditing fees, insurance costs, and other key costs and looked at making changes to reduce our cost structure.

At the same time, the executive team worked on forming a joint venture with a large global partner and we invested in a new plant together. This helped our growth trajectory.

In this case, it was a heart attack situation. The Board was supportive of changing auditors, of changing our insurance brokers, of moving offices, of putting in additional equity, changing our bank because, when we got a line of credit, we had to move our banking.

If you come in as a new CFO and see it's in a full-blown crisis, the bad news is you're in a crisis. The good news is it gives you a burning desire to make a lot of changes very quickly. You continue to touch base with the Board, but they would likely support those changes.

In heart attack situations, you must do everything all at the same time, so in this example I gave you; I changed the auditors, the bank accounts, the line of credit, the corporate office, the staffing, the accounting system, and raised equity and revamped the corporate team, while building a joint venture business, all within 12 months. It was phenomenal speed to go through, but that's what was necessary.

Now if the situation were not as dire, I wouldn't make as many changes as quickly because the organization, frankly, wouldn't tolerate it. If it's not as broken, people are more resistant to making changes. You must quickly get the assessment of how bad it is, how quickly we must act and then go through it again, touching base with the Board, engaging the stakeholders, communicating quick wins.

That's key because, if they see some quick wins, they'll be supportive behind the next change. "Hey, I have to move the corporate offices because it's going to save us money and it's a better location," and people align and support that. When they see the savings, then you can say, "Okay, now I need to change our auditors."

Those aren't casual decisions, but when they see the quick wins, it gives the Board and the CEO confidence the changes you're making are reasonable and for the best of the organization, and they support you to continue making those changes.

Successful Fundraising

Jan: What suggestions do you have for fundraising?

Suzy: Fundraising is a fun activity for me because it tells a story. What potential investors and lenders want to know is the story behind it. The story should be a well-articulated narrative of the strategic plan. Often, it makes sense to do a strategic planning exercise with the Board before launching the fundraising.

Like every good story, they want to know there's a happy ending. "Hey, we need this funding and we're going to invest; the business is going to grow, profitability is going to increase, the return on investment's going to be 30%, 40%, 50%," whatever it is. You want a happy ending. The story has some good characters in it because you like to have strong, interesting characters in a good story.

For an investor or lender, those characters are the employees and the executive team. They want to know, "If we're going to invest in this company or lend to it, who are the strong players?" Who's going to carry the ball and make this success come out?

Tell a Good Story

Like any good story, it should have some challenges in it. As you tell the story, you need to be clear about what you think the challenges are.

- Who are the competitors?
- What are the threats?
- What is the liquidity risk?

And so on. It's important the investors and potential lenders know that you know the business, the new CFO who is asking for this funding understands the business and challenges. If the new CFO doesn't present any challenges or threats and says, "This is going to be a cakewalk," people assume the person doesn't know the business.

It's important to communicate what those challenges are and how we are going to mitigate those risks or overcome them to get buy-in. It's a compelling story and it's credible. To me, fundraising is telling a good story.

Just as any good storyteller needs to know their audience, when doing fundraising, you need to know the audience. That's a critical part of it:

who you ask for money and who's your target. I've been with small startups where it's in early stages, an early startup with no revenue. In this case, funding is coming from angel investors or venture capitalists. At that point, you're not going to go to a big bank and ask for a loan. In extreme, early stages, you're telling a story to the venture capitalists.

On the other extreme, I've been with large; established companies with successful earning history for 10, 20, 30 years. There, you're going to established banks, the risk is much lower, and of course, the borrowing cost is going to be much lower, and they're looking for growth, but the growth they're looking for is more like 3% a year, versus an early stage venture capital investor who's looking for 50% revenue or earnings growth a year.

As a storyteller, you need to know who your audience is and who you're approaching, what kind of risk/return profile they're looking for, you should craft a story to meet their needs.

The CFO's job is to put that story into a financial model. The banks or lenders or investors will always want to see a detailed financial forecast that shows a consistent trend with history. The key assumptions would be clearly articulated and believable. The financial model should show a stretch where the organization is challenging itself. But the objectives should be achievable.

Generally, lenders look for more conservative forecasts. They want 90% or more probability that the company can hit its plan numbers and repay the loan. Equity investors generally prefer more aggressive plans with much higher growth trajectory. Investors are often looking at other comparable investment options and expecting very high rates of return so for this opportunity to rise to the top of their list, it has to compete with other high-risk but high-reward options. I've seen some companies develop two plans. Their base plan which has over 90% probability that they can share with banks. But they also have their high growth case which the management team may target internally.

Experienced CFOs build a relationship with banks, lenders, venture capitalists, private equity firms, investors, and other funding sources so they can understand the audience. The CFO that can bring these strong funding networks can add a lot of value to his or her organization.

I've had the range of experience of financing from a million dollars to two and a half billion dollars. It's always telling a story to your audience, but the story can be very different, and the risk/reward ratio can be very different, depending on which end of the spectrum you're in.

Creating and Maintaining a Partnership with the CEO

Jan: How do you partner with the CEO?

Suzy: I had a CEO who turned to me one day and said, "Take all the cash from the bank." It's an amazing statement if you stop and think about it.

I had been with this CEO for about a year, and we had some problems with our bank accounts. At this point we were frustrated, we were opening a new bank account, but it was taking some time. One day, the CEO got frustrated and said, "Suzy, take all the cash out of the bank." I asked, "Where do I put it?" He replied, "Just put it in your own personal bank account, and once the new bank account is open, we can transfer the money over."

It's amazing to me he said that. He trusted me completely with all the money at the company. Of course, I didn't transfer the funds into my account. I don't want to go there, but it highlights the trust that was built between me and the CEO, and that's what I look for in relationships with CEOs: getting to the point where they completely, absolutely trust me.

Building Trusting Relationships

It's a difficult relationship to build. As a CFO, I constantly think about how to build trust. The CEO must trust the CFO. The CFO signs contracts, sign checks and payments, hires finance team members who have access to cash and payments and much confidential information. The CFO represents the company in numerous public settings. CFOs make a lot of important judgment calls, so trust must be very, very strong.

In studies, I've seen on the relationship between CEOs and CFOs, the longest tenure from CFOs is where the CEOs have said the level of trust is very high. It seems to be the critical number one factor in deciding how the relationship between CEO/CFO is working. That's why sometimes when you see a new CEO come in, they'll bring a new CFO with them if they can't build trust with the existing CFO.

That trust is built in some ways. A good communication dialogue is required. It's aligning on the strategic initiative where the vision of the company is. It's sharing a common style of working together. Is it a very informal CEO? Is it a visionary CEO? Is it a very big-picture or is it detail-of-the-week CEO? This is where the CFO must align and build trust. It's a hard activity. A lot of it comes down to personal skills and the art of friendship. A good relationship would be enjoyable and a friendship, not a working relationship.

It's like a marriage between CEO and CFO. If the relationship works well, it's a wonderful experience. When trust exists, the CFOs are very successful, and the company will also have more successful results.

I'm big on communication. Be on engagement alignment; check in very frequently, say, "I'm doing this. Are you okay with that?" "I see this issue, are you okay with that?" If I find a CEO I can joke around with, we get along much better because it gets you through the tough spots if you can crack a joke now and then and laugh at some sticky situation. If you find a CEO that can say, "Yeah, take all the cash in the bank," you know you have the trust you want.

Jan: What advice do you have, Suzy, if someone doesn't have a good relationship with their CEO? How can they go about repairing it?

Suzy: I think helping the CEO look good helps immensely.

This is a key one where I always make sure the CEO knows I've got their back. I'm constantly thinking, "What can I do to help them? What can I do to make their job easier? What can I do to make them look good?" I always keep in mind it's my job to shine the light, it's their job to shine.

Making the CEO Look Good

Hopefully, what makes a CEO look good is consistent with the vision of the strategic plan.

It becomes difficult if the CEO has a different agenda than the overall shareholders or the Board. In that situation, I think it's a good time to update your resume.

Otherwise, if the CEO is trying to achieve what the Board and the shareholders want, then think about how to make them look good. The CEOs appreciate that. If it's a style thing, I think you can get through that. I change my style sometimes if I find the CEO has a different style. If the CEO is very formal, I can go into a formal style. If the CEO prefers face-to-face meetings, we meet in person. If he or she prefers emails, we communicate through emails. Building a personal relationship helps. One CEO I worked with traveled extensively. I checked her calendar and scheduled to travel with her so we could have face-to-face meetings wherever and whatever time zone she was in. It also helped that I saw the parts of the company she saw and met the same team members and heard the same issues with her. Meeting outside of work with each other's families to make sure there's a bond of friendship, I find really, helps also.

I try to find common ground with people.

I had a CEO who liked eating a lot of different kinds of foods, which was great for me. I was happy to try all kinds of strange foods together. There's a lot of bonding that happens while eating. I think it was goat legs someplace, I got the quail another time, and I had this weird seafood sea urchin thing.

I had another CEO who worked with a lot of music and was a blast. He'd bring all kinds of crazy fun songs and crack me up, funny stuff you can kind of joke and laugh together over. I think it helps a lot.

As CFO, we want to align with the CEO on the key vision and strategy of the company. We want to share the same core values. The personal relationship helps build that bond of trust. If we have a common view on these fundamentals, then an optimistic cheery disposition and sense of humor make for a great long-term partnership.

Selling and Leading Change

Jan: How do you sell and lead change?

Suzy: I like to tell a story about someone who said, "Thanks for volunteering." When I was in college, I was an engineering student, and our college had an annual homecoming event. There was a big parade, and there'd be floats from every department and different organizations. We were at an Engineering Club meeting, and they said, "Oh yeah, there's the annual homecoming event, and there'll be a parade in a couple of months." I said, "Great, so we can have an engineering float." They said, "No, no, no, there's nobody to lead the effort." I said, "We should have an engineering float. It'll show off our department. It's good for morale. It'll be fun!" They said, "Great! Thanks for volunteering, Suzy."

Leadership is Having a Vision

If the new CFO has a vision of where their organization can go and how to get there, if they see a crisis and how to get out of it, or an opportunity and how to take advantage of it, people will naturally fall in line behind them.

This is why the strategic planning process can help give a leadership role to the CFO.

Organizations are always looking for new ideas and someone who's passionate and willing to drive it. In the case of the parade, I volunteered. I said, "Okay, I have no idea, I've never done a float." I called a meeting and a few folks volunteered. We brainstormed some ideas and came up with a plan. Then I called around, got some people to donate money, called different organizations and some friends and said, "Hey if each of you pitches in..." On every call, I would share the vision and why they would want to get involved with it. I got about 60 people to volunteer and put a float together, and we went to the parade.

As a new CFO, I've seen this happen in organizations, too. I don't necessarily come in and say, "Let me lead." I come in and say, "Gosh, we have an opportunity here."

For example, during the 2007 subprime mortgage crisis, I was in an industrial organization, a global company which had been losing money, about $100 million dollars a year for many years. Of course, with the subprime mortgage, the economy was collapsing, and our volume dropped by about 20% in one year. It was a scary time.

I started talking with the executive team, and I said, "You know, we can cut some costs here. We can improve some of our pricing there. Also, when we do close accounting and include the real all-in-cost, we're losing money on some products and customers; we can stop selling products that are losing money and raise prices on some others in more attractive markets, we could more than make up margins." As CFO, you have access to so much data, and you can help give some good advice.

Because I could see the problem and I had a vision for some solution or some ideas, it put me naturally in a leadership position to work with the executive team. We put together a new strategic plan and did some corporate restructuring, reduced some costs, but invested more in some places, changed our pricing, changed our marketing strategy. We went from an organization losing about $100 million a year to making over $500 million a year during the recession, even though the volumes had dropped off.

This is the power of having ideas to contribute. I naturally was volunteered to be the leader.

Stepping Up in a Crisis

A similar situation happened where I was CFO of another company, we had a wonderful CEO, a great man; we were all bereft when he unexpectedly had a stroke. He was in the hospital in crisis mode, we didn't have a COO, we didn't have any other executive positions, it was me and the operations folks.

I stepped up and said, "It's going to be okay. This is our strategic plan. This is the direction we're going in. Here are the metrics we measure ourselves on." I was setting a calm tone and showing we knew where we're going, we knew how to get there, and we were optimistic about it.

The organization naturally follows because people are looking for someone to give a good idea or direction. They look for someone who is optimistic and positive; this inspires the organization to continue forward. In this situation, we were in the process of selling the company. We were able to sell the company successfully. Our CEO eventually recovered. Today he's in great health. He never came back to work full-time, so for the next year and a half, I was leading the organization through that challenging time, and the eventual exit.

Have a vision, have a calm, positive, optimistic voice, and naturally, be volunteered for leadership.

Working Internationally

Jan: How would a CFO adjust the strategies discussed if working in an international setting?

Suzy: The golden rule is "do unto others as you'd have them do unto you," but that doesn't work internationally.

If you're a beef-eater, you may love having a steak dinner, but you wouldn't invite a Hindu colleague to a steakhouse. If you enjoy discussing business over a glass of wine, you wouldn't do this with a Muslim colleague.

These cultural differences also imply significant, less-visible differences in how business is conducted globally. In the US, it's common to bond a construction project at 100%. In Europe, the practice is to bond only 10% of a project. In the US, a bank loan is typically from the bank to the lender with the borrower choosing how/when to use the funds to pay vendors. In China, it's common for the bank to keep the loan funds and to pay the vendors directly, on behalf of the borrower. Accounting rules under IFRS are different from GAAP and can differ from local accounting. For example, as Controller of a foreign subsidiary of a US company, due to differences in goodwill accounting, I reported significant losses for our company under US GAAP but strong profits under local GAAP. Tax rules, interest rates, financing options, banking systems, legal recourses, and accounting rules vary greatly from country to country.

Strategies Same/Application Different

Having worked as CFO of a New Zealand company, a Canadian company, and now a German company, I've learned the general strategies are the same but how they are applied can vary greatly.

Minimizing risk is always a good strategy.

In the US, this may mean keeping surplus cash in a bank account, but in some locations around the world, banks can be unstable. Foreign exchange depreciation can erode the value of local currency, the central bank can restrict convertibility to hard currency, local governments can arbitrarily restrict access to the account or seize it outright, and there can even be taxes on the cash balance (not on interest income but the actual cash balance). In European countries with negative interest rates, the depositor must pay interest to the bank on the bank balance!! In some places, keeping cash in the bank is riskier than keeping cash under the mattress. Detailed due diligence and research will identify these issues. So the strategy to minimize risk is the same strategy but the execution will be different.

The Adjusted Golden Rule

Tarun Khanna presented the concept of "Contextual Intelligence" in his *Harvard Business Review* article of September 2014. Their research showed the success of a company in one country is not at all correlated to the success of the company in another country.

Successful business strategies cannot simply be transported and replicated across the border.

Contextual intelligence means understanding the local context, so the CFO can apply the adjusted golden rule.

Do unto others as they would have done unto themselves.

In many Asian and Latin countries, agreements are based more on the relationship than legal contracts. I've seen joint venture agreements in the US more than a hundred pages. In other countries, the joint venture agreements may be one or two pages. In those situations, it's important to invest time in the relationship and not rely heavily on legal remedies and recourses in the contract.

The Three F's

It becomes more important but also more challenging to build relationships. I've found three Fs to be helpful for initiating friendships and trust in international settings: food, family, and football (soccer, not American football). All three are important anywhere in the world and have helped me start a conversation and form a bond.

Speaking another language is incredibly valuable in building a bridge, so I tried to learn Spanish when working in Latin America. It gave me credibility and helped create valuable and enjoyable personal relationships.

Trustworthy Local Partners

For a new CFO, it's critical to identify trustworthy local partners who can highlight the contextual differences and advise the CFO how to navigate local issues.

He or she cannot assume they can apply the same processes they did back home. Supply chains which are robust and efficient in the US may not operate as efficiently elsewhere. A shipment from Argentina to the US which would usually take one month took six months. The labor laws and culture are different in Argentina, so there were several strikes by the dock workers at the port, which halted shipments.

The key is to understand the risks, reassess expected reward, adjust timelines, and put in place risk mitigation strategies which work locally.

Of course, international locations offer many opportunities not available in the US. Going global is a great growth strategy for a US company having matured in the US market. US companies can tap into new customers and new suppliers as well as new partnerships outside the US.

Non-US markets provide a great diversification strategy. Taking advantage of low-cost manufacturing locations can optimize supply chains. Strong GDP growth rates in many emerging markets are double or triple the growth rates in the US. Internet connectivity has enabled smaller companies in emerging economies to connect to the global economy and get access to processes, tools, practices, and standards of developed countries.

I was surprised to see many companies in Vietnam or the Czech Republic are performing at levels to comparable companies in the US, but with a much lower cost structure. Strategic acquisitions of local companies can allow shortcut access to rapidly growing markets.

CFOs need to embrace the opportunity and challenge of international growth.

Quantifying and Reducing Your Risk

Jan: How do you deal with risk management?

Suzy: I like to share an analogy about my car. In my car, like most cars, it has a gas meter to tell me how much gas is in the tank, and there's a little light that goes on, "Gas is low."

What I love about my car is it doesn't say the gas is low, it says how many more miles you have before you're out of gas.

For me, risk management is all about knowing how many more miles you have before you run out of gas? Quantifying risk.

It's great because if I'm driving the car and the light comes on, I'm not wondering if I have two miles or 50 miles to go. It tells me how many miles, and it keeps track, so I know how much time I have, and if it's urgent to act or I can take my time.

Risk mitigation or risk management, to me, is all about understanding and quantifying risk. How much gas is in the tank and how much longer can I go on it?

How Much Risk is Risky

I think this is where Heffernan is fantastic coming in and doing a risk assessment. I love working with Jan Berthold. She'll tell me, "Here's the risk you have. Here's the risk you have on cybersecurity and comparing and benchmarking it to competitors in the industry." At that point, I have a sense of where we are, if it's risky or if it's high risk or low risk compared to others, what's the impact on my business?

Then I can quantify and make decisions on how to mitigate. I think risk assessment tools fit perfectly with the way I think of risk management, which is to *quantify the risk* and then you decide *how to mitigate it.*

Why don't you share with us what your Risk Assessment is, Jan?

Jan: The Risk Management Assessment is an analysis we do - we take all the insurance policies and read every page. We identify and prioritize risk, evaluate the safety and risk management policies of the company, as well as the procedures. We do a claims review and analysis, and come back with an action plan for improvement. In one of Suzy's companies, they had very strong worker's comp results, so we didn't have too much to change there.

On the other hand, we found other errors in places where they were over insured or underinsured, and there were errors in the policies. Things were missing. Things were out of date. It's kind of death by a thousand cuts; lots of sloppy mistakes are often made and discovered.

It's hard for CFOs because they don't have time to read every page of the policy. They're not insurance experts, and you don't know what you don't know. It's a good way for them, like Suzy said, to look good at the company. We can show ways to save money and correct errors.

We benchmark what they're paying compared with other companies in their SIC code, what their limits are, what coverages they have, what they might not have. It's a way to give more visibility to risk management.

Suzy: It's a fantastic tool. It goes back to my comment about making quick wins. Heffernan and Jan's team put together a great risk assessment book for us in the company. I shared it with the Board, and said, "We worked with Heffernan and put together this great risk assessment, and they're making recommendations, I'm suggesting we take these actions on risk mitigation."

The Board loved it. It was backed by comparison and experience from Heffernan looking at other competitors and industry standards. This had not been done in this company before. As I said, you made me look good. It got a lot of good support and quick buy-in from the Board, so it was really, successful for us.

The Risk Management Assessment

Suzy Taherian recommends CFOs get some early wins with a company. The Risk Management Assessment will provide a quick win for the new CFO or validate the current situation for long-term CFOs.

Using our unique assessment, we can eliminate errors and overcharges in the insurance program and position the company as a very attractive risk to the carrier. This results in not only better pricing, but also better terms and conditions at renewal.

I started doing Risk Management Assessments in 2000 after reading an article by Scott Addis of the Addis Group. Shortly after that, I met with a CFO who validated the process for me. I was excited to meet with this CFO because I had an insurance market no one else had, so I talked on and on about how I could save him money. He interrupted me and said, "Insurance is a pain in the blankety-blank, but if there is ever a claim that is not covered, it could be catastrophic for the company." And catastrophic for his career.

He told me my job was to let him know of all the company's exposures, so, if there is a claim not covered, he is off the hook. It was an "*aha*" moment for me. Together, we did a Risk Management Assessment where we found key errors on certain policies. For example, they were paying a $37,000 premium for insurance on a lease which they did not have to pay because the insurance was paid for by the landlord.

We got a refund on the lease and corrected the errors on the policy which saved them 14% on their premium. The CFO looked like a hero. Ever since then, I have been doing Risk Management Assessments with great success.

During the Risk Management Assessment, we review all insurance policies, company procedures, and training. We also do one-on-one interviews with key employees of the organization, with the CEO being interviewed last because his or her thoughts on risk issues are likely the most important. Interviews typically take 10 to 15 minutes each. At the end of the process, we present a report which summarizes the results.

Typically, the report includes:

- A review of our process
- Analysis of the current policies and coverages, highlighting any errors or areas needing improvement
- Benchmarking of limits and premium for companies in the same SIC code
- Claims review and analysis
- An implementation plan for improvement.

We do not charge for the Risk Management Assessment; we consider it an investment in building a trusted-advisor relationship. The assessments can take anywhere from 30 to 50 hours of our time, so we are very selective with whom we work.

If you'd like to see if you are a fit, call me at 650-842-5205 or email me at **Janiceb@heffins.com**.

Here's How to Make Strategic Transformations in Your Company

What makes one CFO able to make lasting and sustainable transformations inside an organization, whereas other CFOs struggle to make a difference?

One of the biggest challenges for a new CFO is often there's not a job description. It's usually something vague along the lines of "Make the CEO look good and help the company succeed". How do you do that, exactly? This book is unlike any other of its kind. We've cut to the chase and shared with the new CFO what they need to do *and* how to do it.

It's said CFOs hold one of the loneliest positions in the executive suite. This perception is by design because the CFO is the counterbalance; the police, and steward of the organization, so the role naturally pits them against others in the organization.

So where can CFOs go for support and actionable insights to overcome the challenges they will face?

That's where this book comes in.

This book helps CFOs get alignment and build relationships with key stakeholders, so they're seen as a guiding force for transformation.

Often there isn't a lot of time to be successful. CFOs are expected to make significant changes and impact in the first 90 days, which means you must hit the ground running.

Contained within this book are little-known shortcuts a new CFO can immediately focus on to bring about the credibility and relationship trust needed to create change within the organization.

About the Authors

Suzy Taherian has more than 20 years of experience as a senior executive for international industrial companies. She started her career with Exxon and Chevron and transitioned to CFO of a mid-size company. She is currently CFO of Kinetics, a global engineering, and construction company specializing in high-purity processing facilities for micro-electronics and biopharma facilities.

As CFO and acting-CEO, she has shaped the strategic vision of many companies and developed detailed plans to achieve turnaround and profitable growth. Her successes include over $4 billion in financings, $2 billion in M&A transactions and successful exits for venture-backed or private-equity backed companies. As CFO of a publicly-traded company, she engineered a shareholder return of 30% in one year.

She has been an adjunct professor at UC Davis Graduate School of Management for the last eight years, teaching courses on International Finance and International Business.

Suzy holds a BS in Mechanical Engineering from UC Davis and an MBA from the Kellogg School of Management, Northwestern University. She serves on several boards. She enjoys living in the Bay Area with her husband and their two intelligent and active teenagers.

Janice Berthold is a Senior Vice-President with Heffernan Insurance Brokers. She is one of the few brokers who work with clients on a "Referral Only" basis.

Prior to merging her firm with Heffernan, Janice was President and CEO of J. Berthold Insurance Service Inc. and a Principal of All West Insurance Brokers, one of the top five closely-held insurance brokerage firms in Silicon Valley.

She has more than 25 years of commercial insurance experience and holds the insurance designations of Professional Workers' Compensation Advisor, Chartered Property Casualty Underwriter, Chartered Life Underwriter, and Chartered Financial Consultant.

She has been an Advisor for the California State Senate Committee on Insurance and is a featured writer for *Business Journal.*

In 1999, she was named Small Business Owner of the Year by the *San Jose Mercury News* and the Women's Fund. In addition, *The Business Journal* named her Enterprising Woman of the Year in 2003.

Janice is a graduate of the University of San Francisco. She sits on the Santa Clara University Board of Fellows, and the Housing Industry Forum Board of Advisors.

Janice lives in Saratoga with her husband Tom and enjoys hiking and reading.

Made in the USA
Coppell, TX
22 August 2021

60988795R00046